A QUICK GUIDE TO

Making Your Teaching Stick

K–5

Other Books in the Workshop Help Desk Series

A Quick Guide to
Reaching Struggling Writers, K–5
M. COLLEEN CRUZ

A Quick Guide to
Teaching Persuasive Writing, K–2
SARAH PICARD TAYLOR

A Quick Guide to
Boosting English Acquisition in Choice Time, K–2
ALISON PORCELLI AND CHERYL TYLER

For more information about these and other titles,
visit www.firsthand.heinemann.com.

A QUICK GUIDE TO
Making Your Teaching Stick
K–5

SHANNA SCHWARTZ

Workshop Help Desk Series
Edited by Lucy Calkins
with the Teachers College Reading and Writing Project

HEINEMANN
Portsmouth, NH

An imprint of Heinemann
361 Hanover Street
Portsmouth, NH 03801–3912
www.heinemann.com

Offices and agents throughout the world

Library of Congress Cataloging-in-Publication Data
Schwartz, Shanna.
  A quick guide to making your teaching stick, K–5 / Shanna Schwartz.
      p. cm. — (Workshop help desk series)
  Includes bibliographical references.
  ISBN 13: 978–0–325–02596–4
  ISBN 10: 0–325–02596–7
  1. Elementary school teaching. 2. Effective teaching. I. Title.
  LB1555.S255 2008
  372.1102—dc22   2008027306

SERIES EDITOR: *Lucy Calkins and the Teachers College Reading and Writing Project*
EDITOR: *Kate Montgomery*
PRODUCTION: *Elizabeth Valway*
COVER DESIGN: *Jenny Jensen Greenleaf*
COVER PHOTO: *Peter Cunningham*
INTERIOR DESIGN: *Jenny Jensen Greenleaf*
COMPOSITION: *House of Equations, Inc.*
MANUFACTURING: *Steve Bernier*

Printed in the United States of America on acid-free paper
12 11 10 09 08 VP 1 2 3 4 5

to my husband

CONTENTS

ACKNOWLEDGMENTS

As a new teacher, I was invited to participate in a meeting at Teachers College that Lucy Calkins was convening to talk about literacy in the kindergarten classroom. I was exhilarated by the invitation but terrified to talk. When I got to the meeting, Lucy and a host of accomplished educators sat around a well-worn wooden table. From the moment the meeting began, people were disagreeing and voicing strong opinions. Lucy took copious notes on a pink legal pad, occasionally slowing the flow of the debate to record competing ideas, even when they differed from her own. I must have looked horrified, because when the group took a quick break about an hour into the meeting, Lucy walked briskly over to me. "This is how we learn," she said quietly but quickly. "We look for the trouble—the hard parts. And then we talk and argue and listen and talk some more. You will see."

I have seen. Now as a member of the Teachers College Reading and Writing Project, I look forward to exchanges like these that push my thinking, help me outgrow my ideas, and teach me to embrace the hard parts because that is where we find our truest understanding. Often the competing ideas bare the greatest insights. Thank you, Lucy, for making me a part of such a hearty group of thinkers.

Of course, that hearty group of thinkers are the coauthors of this book. Thank you to all of the members of the TCRWP for teaching and pushing and learning alongside me. Especially, I want to thank Amanda Hartman, who is one of the most generous teachers I know. Thank you to Ellen Ellis, who tried so much of this work. And of course I must thank the teachers and administrators from the schools with which I work most closely: P.S. 59, P.S. 18, P.S. 188, Roosevelt Elementary, Willits Elementary, Sickles Elementary School, the members of my leadership group and specialty course; the pages of this book are filled with the knowledge we have constructed together—thank you for learning with me.

I want to thank Julia Mooney. I fear you have read this text more often than I have, and I thank you. As a writing mentor and friend, you have been wise and helpful and lovely—all writers need a Julia! And to Kate Montgomery, thank you for this opportunity; it has been a thrill for me.

Finally, I want to thank my family. Thank you to my husband, who helped me find the time to write and then reminded me that I knew how; to my father, who read and edited and cheered me on; to my mother, who knew what it was like to feel stuck and then helped me through; and to my children: Lila, who allowed me to nurse her and type at the same time, and Judah, who moaned, "Mama, I don't want you to write your book—I want you to play." All I can say is "Let's *play*!"

INTRODUCTION

As a Teachers College Reading and Writing Project staff developer, I travel from school to school and give workshop after workshop to hundreds of teachers. Always, we talk about the successes and difficulties of workshop teaching. Without fail, after the initial concerns are articulated, as we dig into the underlying issues that animate them, the teachers lean in as if to whisper, and—in one way or another—they say, "What I really want to know most is how do I make my teaching *stick*?"

There is good reason for this question. As teachers, we gather children together each day, teach them a clear and concise strategy, give them a concrete example of that teaching, often drawing on stories from our own or their lives, and watch them nod their heads and smile—only to later find them oblivious to that day's teaching point, blithely repeating what they've done the day before.

Somehow, though we carefully plan our teaching, though we practice and revise it with our colleagues, it often doesn't transfer to children's independent work. We teach and children get it, but they do not *hold onto* what they've learned. And we're left wishing we had a way to pin the lesson to children's shirts and make it stay forever.

It is for this reason that even the most successful teachers always want to know, "How do I make my teaching *stick*?"

This book stands on the shoulders of the TCRWP. It is an extension of Lucy Calkins' *Units of Study for Primary Writing* (Calkins et al. 2003). It reflects our newest thinking about how we can get the teaching we do with our youngest learners to last. We at the TCRWP not only continually outgrow our *own* best thinking but also draw on the thinking of the authors, teachers, coaches, and educational leaders with whom we work. The ideas about "stickiness" here draw from the writing and thinking of many authors: Lev Vygotsky, Jerome Bruner, Donald Graves, Gravity Goldberg and Jennifer Serravallo, Stephanie Parsons, and Georgia Heard. This book gathers that collective thinking in one place and clearly lays out principles and practices that underlie stickiness. It explores how to tweak our teaching so that it has a more lasting impact on our writers.

This book also stands on the shoulders of a best-selling book that is not traditionally cited in the field of education: Malcolm Gladwell's *Tipping Point* (2002). In this momentous book, Gladwell talks about how some things in the world have amazing spreading and staying power. These things have what he names the "stickiness factor." To write his book, Gladwell scoured the world, finding examples from all walks of life. He discovered that much of what makes one thing stick also makes another stick; in short, there is universality to stickiness.

It's not surprising, then, that much of what makes good teaching stick is the same as what makes *anything* stick. *Naming* these principles, laying them out in one guide on how to make our teaching endure, is the goal of this book.

The text draws on the ideas of teachers and theorists alike. From this information, I have delineated four stickiness principles, which inform the practical teaching methods offered throughout this book.

CHAPTER ONE

The Stickiness Principles

Are there smaller, subtler, easier ways to make something stick?
—MALCOLM GLADWELL

Children, like all humans, do not just learn things whole and then do those things perfectly from that day on, forever. Humans learn through a start-and-stop process that frequently involves (partially) learning something and losing it and then—we hope—learning it again and trying to do it as an approximation, and maybe learning it again, until it finally sticks. One of our jobs as teachers is to provide the numerous iterations needed for a lesson to stick, thus helping children move through the approximation period into solid comprehension and use of a new concept.

Making our teaching stick—more often or with more students—therefore requires a good understanding of the normal process of learning and losing knowledge and a good understanding of why, where, and when the four stickiness principles work.

First, let me name these stickiness principles plainly:

▶ Children's engagement and learning are dependent on a high level of understanding; they are distracted most when their understanding breaks down. In order for teaching to stick, children need to be taught what they are *ready* to learn.

▶ Children learn best when they are *engaged and active* participants in their own learning. In our minilessons, we can create engagement in three major ways: by telling little stories to connect our teaching to their lives; by using gestures that get their bodies active; and by asking them to act and to role-play.

▶ Children may show great interest in our teaching, but if they don't have something to remind them of that teaching later, they often forget it. We need to provide physical representations of our teaching for children to hold onto as they apply their newfound knowledge.

▶ Children learn through—and love—*repetition*. We need to use the power of repetition to create situations where children approximate and accumulate greater and greater understanding.

Let's explore these further by examining each principle and defining the role of each principle in turning our lessons into our students' habits.

Children Learn What They Are *Ready* to Learn

Children are more attentive and learn more when they understand more. Most people associate this principle with Lev Vygotsky (1978), who said we learn best when the new material is in our "zone of proximal development"—that is, by determining that which the child can do with just a little help or repetition, we can determine not only what he knows now but also what he will learn next. According to Vygotsky, "The zone of proximal development defines those functions that have not yet matured but are in the process of maturation, functions that will mature tomorrow but are currently in an embryonic state" (86). The idea of the ZPD implies that if we can determine what a child is ready to learn and then teach that, we will have her closest attention. Therefore, our work becomes determining our students' ZPD and then teaching material that falls within that zone of understanding. In other words, when the lesson adds only a manageable quantum of new material to what our students already understand, our teaching stays with them—it sticks.

In order to teach within children's zone of proximal development, we can draw on two overarching concepts:

▶ We can think about any skill as a ladder, that is, we need to be able to imagine what a child does at an emergent level, what he does as he becomes more skilled, and so on. Our teaching aims to help students acquire increasingly sophisticated writing strategies one incremental element at a time. Our goal is not the ultimate; if we were teaching perfection, we'd probably be reaching too far or trying to have students acquire too many new ideas in one lesson.

▶ We can aim to create learning scaffolds, through which we provide heavy support at first, then remove this support one small element at a time. This allows learners to acquire the whole writing strategy in an incremental way. That is, in order to help a learner move along the line of growth, we release scaffolds as the child moves toward using the skill with increasing independence.

Let's look more closely at each of the stickiness principles, exploring how each principle applies to teaching writing to K–2 youngsters.

Children Learn Best When They Are *Engaged and Active* Participants in Their Own Learning

Engagement is key to making teaching stick. The challenge is to both *get* and *keep* children's attention. In this book we'll look at how to *get* children engaged by using stories—stories about ourselves, our classrooms, our students. Jerome Bruner, author of the foundational book *The Process of Education*, says that children "turn things into stories, and when they try to make sense of their lives they use the storied version of their experience as a basis for further reflection. If they don't catch things in narrative structure, it doesn't get remembered very well" (1999, 56).

Next, we will consider how to *keep* children engaged through movement and play. "Physical movement actually has an inordinate amount of impact on creating and accessing memory. . . . *Movement helps cement memory!"* (Jones 1999, 1). Kids love few things more than wiggling their bodies, making meaningful hand gestures, and acting out roles, and we can draw on this propensity to not sit still to help them learn.

Here are some methods we use to engage children:

- *Using stories to draw in our learners.* Stories can be a powerful connector between our children and the strategies we want to teach them.

- *Using gestures to create gross motor memory.* This can help strategies stick with students even after the lesson is over. Using the same gestures throughout the day can also remind and coach students to carry the strategies that they use during writing time across the curriculum, thus solidifying the strategies.

- *Using role-playing and acting to move children from talking about strategies to trying them on their own.* Pretending is a natural part of young children's lives, and we can use their ability to pretend to help them play their way into writing with feeling and clarity.

Children Benefit from *Physical Representations* of Their Learning

Just as they benefit from being physical *learners*, children also benefit from having access to physical *objects* related to their learning. Adults who are learning something new often take notes to cement our learning. These notes are a way of keeping us attentive as we learn and a way of recalling important information when we need it. In taking notes, we turn the words of the presenter into signs and symbols we can use to recall the information later. Why does this work? Vygotsky explains it this way: "When a human being ties a knot in her handkerchief as a reminder, she is, in essence, constructing the process of memorizing by forcing an external object to remind her of something; she transforms remembering into an external activity. . . . The very essence of human memory consists in the fact that human beings actively remember with the help of signs" (1978, 51).

Note taking, however, does not work for our youngest children. Our five-, six-, and seven-year-old students simply don't yet have the writing skills to take notes that would help. In fact, if we asked children to take notes as they learned, they would spend all their energy figuring out how and what to write and would therefore have no energy left for learning the concept or idea we were teaching. So what do we do? As Vygotsky suggests, we can help children by making notes and representations for and with them. Most teachers make poster-size charts and hope these serve as physical representations of learning.

Charts are fantastic classroom tools because they create a sign to help children remember, but they work only if we make an effort to be sure they are memorable! Often they are not in children's faces enough to help them implement new ideas. Just as advertisers use a diversity of media to get their ideas to stick with consumers, we need to do the same in our classrooms. We will explore ways to create more accessible and memorable variations of the classroom chart, so that children

understand charts in the moment and can access that understanding again and again as needed. We will do this through
two main methods:

- using pictures, photographs, catchphrases, and student
  work to help children hold onto our teaching
- using folder-size charts and individual cards that can be
  customized to remind different children to use different skills and strategies, drawn from the larger whole-
  class charts

Children Learn Through—and Love—*Repetition*

The principle of repetition is not altogether new to those of us
who teach. This is the ZPD at work! We realize that learning
is not linear, that there is always a period in which we are *trying* to do something, but not necessarily doing it with success.
Even more important, learning and forgetting, which we so
often witness, is actually a symptom of nonlinearity. Often, as
teachers, we are frustrated by this. But children don't truly forget what we have taught; they just have not yet learned to
apply it yet. If we want them to apply the learning, we need
to give them time. Repetition is the most important process
through which we can translate time into learning.

Successful repetition in the classroom is more complicated
than teaching the same lesson twice. It involves a degree of
sophistication and variation. We can use repetition in four
contexts:

- in the minilesson
- inside the unit
- from unit to unit
- throughout the day

A Sticky Minilesson

There are many ways to apply the four major principles in our teaching, and certainly any minilesson can encompass each of the principles. In the following example, the teacher has carefully crafted a minilesson that applies each principle. In each of the following chapters, we will take a closer look at how she does this.

Connection

The teacher began, "Writers, remember how on Monday, Jordan shared a picture from his all-about book with us during the share? We were so impressed with how much he taught us in a single picture." The teacher held up Jordan's picture. "Remember how Anna took one look at it and said, 'I didn't know that dolphins had teeth!' We decided that authors of all-about books use small details in the pictures to teach more information. After looking at Jordan's piece, we started to notice how much the pictures in many of your books taught.

"Yesterday, many of you worked so hard to make your pictures detailed so they could teach readers. When I walked over to Desiree, she gave me a little quiz. She said, 'I put four things you can learn in this picture. Can you find them?' It was funny. But then I could only find three things, and Desiree had to show me the last one. But you know what? That Desiree is one smart cookie! Before I left, she put labels in her picture and drew arrows to different items on it so as to make sure her reader could find everything she was teaching. Take a look." The teacher held up the page from Desiree's book.

"Today, I want to teach you that we all can be like Desiree. When we, as writers, want to be sure that our readers learn all the things we hope to teach in a picture, we can add labels with arrows."

Teach

The teacher continued, "Let's take a look at this mural we made in science when we wanted to teach people about our pet iguana, Beatrice. Do you remember how we first drew the general stuff, and then for lots of days, different children worked on the mural, adding specific details? For example, DaQuan added a squash flower, making it over the iguana's head. That wasn't just a pretty picture, was it? You were adding information; you were teaching people that iguanas eat flowers and other plants. It *could* be, though, that some people will miss your lesson! So, watch me as I add labels with arrows to make sure that the reader will notice the important information you guys added." The teacher and each child put a finger to their eye to show that they were watching. This is a gesture they agreed upon to indicate that they are watching something.

"Let's see. I know DaQuan added the squash flower hoping people would learn from this detail, so I'll add an arrow and write what DaQuan wants the people to learn. Hmm . . . I could say just one word: 'food.' Or I could say, 'Flowers and plants are Iguana food' (so they know it's not *just* squash flowers that iguanas eat).

"Hmm . . . what else? Well, here is her water; she needs it for bathing and drinking. I could label that." The teacher wrote "water for baths and drink" and then drew an arrow to the water.

"Writers, did you notice that I studied the picture, found a detail that we hope will teach, then made a label with an arrow and wrote a couple words to help readers learn the information?"

Active Engagement

"Now it is your turn to try. Remember, look closely at the picture, find something we can teach people about Beatrice, and think about the label you would add with an arrow." The teacher put her finger to her temple and made a "thinking face." The children did the same.

"When you have an idea about something important to label, put a quiet thumb on your knee." Thumbs popped up right away. "Turn to your partner and share your ideas." Children chattered away for a bit and the teacher called them back quickly.

"Great, you have a lot of ideas! Noya, will you share your thought?"

"We can put 'rock' on there."

"What does 'rock' teach the reader about our iguana? Is it important to notice?"

"Yeah, 'cause she scratches her claws on the rock to make them sharp!" Other children nodded vigorously.

"Great! So you want to teach people that iguanas use rocks to sharpen their claws. Come on up and add that. You could even write 'rock for claws'."

"While Noya writes her label the teacher went on, "whisper to the child next to you to point out another label that we can add." The students talked to their partners again.

"Thumbs up if you have an idea." Students turned their attention back to the teacher, and Noya returned to her spot on the rug. "Daisean, what were you thinking?"

"We can write 'screen' at the top because that lets the light in! Iguanas need light to live."

"Great, come on up!"

Daisean added the label.

"Fabulous! You all did a great job of looking closely at the picture, finding something important to teach readers about our iguana, and thinking about the label you would add with an arrow."

Link

"So, writers, I am going to take this newly labeled mural of Beatrice's habitat and put it on this chart." The teacher taped the picture onto an already titled piece of chart paper.

She pointed as she read the title of the chart. "'Ways to Make Our Pictures Teach More.' First, we need to list the strategy of adding lots of details to the picture. I'll write,

'Details, Details, Details.' Since we like to be able to act out our strategies, let's act that out like this." The teacher tapped her index finger to her thumb, then her middle finger to her thumb, and then her ring finger. As the children tried the motion, the teacher wrote, "Details, Details, Details," at the bottom and circled a few details in the mural to illustrate the idea.

"Now I want to write the strategy that we learned today: label information with an arrow. What would be a fun way to act that out?" The teacher paused to think, and children started to whisper. Finally the teacher looked up and made eye contact with Sam.

"We could just draw an arrow with our fingers in the air," he suggested. Immediately, a few children started to mime drawing an arrow. The teacher smiled and quickly wrote, "Label information with an arrow," on the chart. She drew an arrow to an example of this on the picture.

"Now let's read our chart together."

The students joined in as their teacher read and pointed to the chart. "'Ways to Make Our Pictures Teach More: Details, Details, Details.'" The children mimed this with their hands.

"'Label information with an arrow.'" The children mimed this also.

"So, writers, anytime you want to add more information to your pictures, you can add details like you have been doing *and* you can use labels with arrows to point out your details. Off you go!"

As children got started, the teacher moved the chart so children would be able to see it while sitting in their seats.

FIG. 1.1 *In the model minilesson, the teacher makes a chart with a small version of the students' mural and then circles the parts in the mural that illustrate the strategy.*

■   ■   ■   ■   ■

"I thought I taught that!" All of us have said this more times than we can count and know the feeling that runs through our bodies as we see children struggle to do something that we thought we had taught so well. This book will give you ideas and suggestions for making your teaching stick with your children and thus make the all-important turn from new concept to writing habit. Some of the ideas will be new to you, and as you apply them you will see that they can be applied in math and reading as well as writing. Other suggestions may not feel entirely new; you'll see that many of the smart methods you are already using can be applied in new ways that will have a greater impact on your students. Go ahead—get sticky!

CHAPTER TWO

Principle 1

Children Learn What They Are Ready to Learn

Kids don't watch when they are stimulated and look away
when they are bored. They watch when they understand
and look away when they are confused.

—MALCOLM GLADWELL

One time my brother, a trained chef, taught me the recipe for a fancy spaghetti sauce. I wanted to do something special for my overworked husband. Josh said, "You could add a half a cup of red wine to give your sauce a greater depth of flavor." Fabulous! Depth of flavor is just what I wanted! Off I went to cook the meal.

Full of anticipation, I chopped the onions and garlic, cooked them in oil, as usual, then added in the half cup of wine. I had never cooked with wine before—this felt very sophisticated.

Later that evening, I forked out the spaghetti and meatballs, a smile on my face. But from the first bite, something was wrong—the noodles tasted like they'd been drenched in wine. Rob and I looked at each other. "What happened?" Rob asked. "Josh told me that wine would give it flavor!" I said, confused. We tossed the disaster of a meal and ordered Chinese.

After dinner, I called my brother and discovered the problem. The wine had to reduce before the tomatoes were added. "I guess I should have told you that . . . ," my brother apologized, "I thought you knew."

We learn best what we are *ready* to learn. My brother's instruction for using wine in red sauce would have been fine if I had cooked with wine before. An experienced cook knows that you always let wine reduce when you cook with it; it didn't occur to Josh that he would need to mention that step. My brother's teaching was two steps ahead of what I was ready to learn, and thus it did not work.

When teaching does not take hold, it is often out of reach for students. This is especially important for teachers to consider when evaluating student growth. Many times standards and curricula lay out what children *need* to learn (perhaps by the end of the year), and knowing the goal can be helpful. But it can also be distracting, because our teaching needs to be influenced especially by knowledge of what particular children are ready to learn. Problems arise when the content and skills we need to teach do not match what most children are *ready* to learn. It's important for teachers to assess children *first* and then fit the curriculum to their needs.

Of course, we all need to do formal assessments of our writers throughout the year. But in order to teach well, we need to also do informal assessments every day. By watching our students and reading their writing, we can discover both what they are doing with relative ease and also what they are trying to do.

One year, as I prepared to write report cards, I reread my conference notes for Kami. They revealed that for six weeks in a row I had talked with Kami about adding spaces to her writing. I had tried six different strategies to teach her to do this. Then I opened her writing folder and saw that she still was not writing with spaces between her words. She was not *using* spaces; she was not *trying* to use spaces; she was not *ready* to use spaces. I needed to teach a skill Kami was *ready* to learn.

A child who is ready to learn something will exhibit signs of this readiness in her writing. One sign of learning readiness is *using but confusing*. This phrase, coined by phonics and spelling guru Donald Bear, refers to the appearance of something in a student's work that the child has tried to do but is not yet doing conventionally. When a child puts a period at the end of each line of her text, she is using but confusing end punctuation—a good indicator that teaching her end punctuation is apt to pay off. In fact, a child like this is a lot like me trying to cook with wine. I was ready to give it a go. I just needed a little more support—a few extra tips—to do it correctly.

When children are using but confusing something, it usually means they are ready to learn more about the skill or strategy they are trying. This phase of approximation can help us choose teaching that will be especially strong and sticky because it will meet students where they are.

Teaching Big Skills While Meeting Children at Their Readiness Points

Almost any skill can be taught in a manner that will make it accessible to young children. For example, most people would probably agree that kindergartners are not ready to learn to draw with perspective. David McGreevy, an art teacher at P.S. 116, thinks differently. He thinks that his challenge as an art teacher is to find a way to talk about the beginning steps underlying drawing with perspective so that young children can begin to experience this important concept. Every year, he gathers a new batch of children in the art room and says, "I've noticed that when you draw pictures of your classrooms or your apartments or your grandmothers' houses, you all use the bottom of the paper as the floor in the drawing. This makes it hard for you to put a lot of details into your picture because only a few things fit on the floor. Today I want to teach you that you can draw a line in the middle of your page to create the floor. Everything above that line will be the walls and everything below it will be the floor. This will give you a lot more room to add to your drawings, okay? This is called adding perspective to your drawing. Artists work on perspective all the time." The children ooh and aah over the examples he holds up and then run to their seats to try it. Perspective is a revolution for kindergartners. The transformation is remarkable. The children's new drawings are far more sophisticated and hold much greater detail.

On this first day and over the course of many weeks in art class, David talks with his students and watches how they put this new concept to work. To start, some children draw the line in the middle of the page and then work hard to understand how that makes the floor bigger. Other children draw the line and see immediately how empowering this is, quickly adding more and more to their pictures. As he works with each child individually, David teaches some how to see the horizon line and move their details all through the bottom half of the page; in essence, he coaches them to use the tip he has just taught. With children who understand the horizon line right away, he teaches more, such as how to make some objects small, thus showing that they are farther away in the background. Each new tip that he offers builds from the work that each child is doing, so he is moving the students along a continuum of understanding, starting where each child is on that first day. In the following years, he returns to the concept of perspective, helping students develop a more complex grasp of it. In fact, over the course of six years—kindergarten through fifth grade—David is the children's art teacher, and he builds on their understanding of perspective each year, pushing each child to try new tips that will make the perspective in their drawings more and more sophisticated. By fifth grade, the students have a much stronger grasp of perspective than most of their classroom teachers.

In order to teach from a person's readiness point, it helps to think about the development of a skill as a spiral. Vygotsky puts it this way: "Development, as often happens, proceeds not as a circle but in a spiral, passing through the same point at each new revolution while advancing to a higher level" (1978, 56).

David's simple tip to put a line in the middle of the page allows young children to work on the big concept of perspective. Children, like anyone learning something new, vary in their levels of acquisition. Our job as teachers is to discover where children are along this spiral of acquisition and to meet them there. Just as David does, we need to teach big concepts and then differentiate our instruction to meet children at their starting points, giving them tips along the way to deepen their ability to work with that concept or skill.

Drawing on a Small Tip to Teach a Big Skill

The stickiest minilessons meet children at their readiness point by conveying a big skill and a small tip. The most effective teaching is big enough to allow for varying degrees of sophistication but still fits with little kids. Let's take a look at how the model minilesson in Chapter 1 does this. In that lesson, the teaching point is *We can write labels with arrows to point out important information to make sure the reader learns a lot from our pictures*. This teaching point is both big and small. It is big enough that we see evidence of the strategy in adult books. In fact, photographers and illustrators work hard to ensure the pictures they contribute to books teach a great deal. The authors and publishers of these texts then work hard to make the words that accompany those pictures point out the most important information the pictures convey.

The teaching point is also small. While the skill—including and pointing out lots of information in a picture—is big, the teacher also gives a small tip: make a label and an arrow. This simple tip allows children to do big work in a small way.

Another lesson that does this particularly well is Revealing Internal Stories from "Small Moments" in *Units of Study for Primary Writing* (Calkins et al. 2003). In this lesson, Lucy Calkins gathers children together and points out that Tatyana has done a really smart thing. She not only wrote her actions but also added her feelings. She described sitting on her mother's lap and then wisely added, "I felt so comfy." Then Lucy goes on to name this very doable, concrete action— adding feelings—in a way that brings out the bigness of what Tatyana has done. Lucy says, "Tatyana has not only told the external story—the actions one can see—she's also told the internal story—the feelings that aren't visible to the outside reader." She names this simply by saying, "She's written not only the external but also the internal story" (94).

This lesson is big. Great novelists do a more sophisticated version of revealing internal stories. James Baldwin, a great American novelist, is famous for his ability to write the internal story. Baldwin writes about racism and homophobia all through the thoughts and feelings of his characters. Revealing the internal stories of characters is at the heart of what makes any writing, at any level, rich. This strategy is right for primary students because Lucy and Abby Oxenhorn give them a manageable way to do something very big.

So, how can you be sure that the strategy you teach is big enough and small enough at the same time? First, you need to ask yourself, "Do adult authors really do this?" If they do, chances are your children will be able to grow inside the strategy.

Let's look at another teaching point: planning a story. Do adult authors do this? Sure they do. Some write outlines and others make time lines, but in one way or another, they plan. If your strategy meets this criterion, you are off to a good start.

When you plan to teach a big skill, ask yourself: "Can I give my children a small tip that will help them do this?" For the minilesson on planning to write, you might tell the students that they can plan by telling their story to a friend or by sketching the story across the pages of a booklet. This would give your young students a way to do grown-up work.

Choosing a whole-class teaching point that has room for growth and then giving children a tip that can help them try this skill is one of the best ways that we can meet our children where they are. By putting big teaching in the small package of a minilesson, we give our children the opportunity to try out our teaching in a simple way. See some more big skills and small tips that Calkins and her colleagues convey in *Units of Study* (2003) in the chart on page 23.

Create Skill Ladders to Differentiate Teaching as You Confer

Once you have taught a minilesson, confer with your writers, helping them turn your teaching into writing. You will notice different children are trying a strategy in different ways. The goal is to help students move to increasingly sophisticated levels inside of any strategy they are trying. The problem is that we often try to move children by leaps and bounds, and when we do this, we lose them. One way to prevent ourselves from doing this is to create and use skill ladders.

Big Skills	Small Tips
Stretch out a word slowly to hear and record the sound of it.	Say it slow like a turtle.
Focus your writing.	Find the most important page of your book and rewrite it so this time you tell it step-by-step.
Punctuation can alter the way a person reads a text.	Use dot, dot, dot (ellipses) to show that time passes, and something will happen soon.
Stretch your stories out.	Write the story across the pages of a booklet.
Develop the important aspect of your story.	Find the most important page and tell more, making that page longer.

A skill ladder is simply a list of ways that a writer can try out a skill. The ladder's lowest rungs are the simplest ways to apply the skill and the higher rungs are the more sophisticated strategies. Just like David walked around his art room, giving different children different tips for working with perspective, you can give your children tips for their writing. You can make your own skill ladders for many skills. Simply take a skill, let's say planning a story, and then make a list of all the possible tips you could imagine perhaps teaching to help children do that skill:

▶ Tell the story to someone.
▶ Sketch the story across the pages of a booklet.
▶ Tell the story to yourself.

- ❱ Tell the story across your fingers, putting out another finger every time something happens.
- ❱ Tell the story as you touch the pages of a booklet.
- ❱ Write key words across the pages of a booklet.
- ❱ Make a time line or an outline of what you plan to say.

After you make your list, start to cluster the tips by difficulty. Many tips will be of equal difficulty, and others will be more or less sophisticated. Put them in a temporary order.

You may find that you do not have a lot of tips for a particular skill. This can pose a challenge for your teaching. So get some help. Ask colleagues about the tips they teach and add those to your ladder. You can also watch your children; they have their own ways of doing things and these are often the most effective. Having a lot of tips for one skill allows you to offer students more rungs on the ladder toward obtaining a skill and thus increases the likelihood that the child will be able to get some footing and to make some progress. No student will need all of these strategies, and we do not suggest teaching them all. Instead, the ladder is meant to give you possibilities.

As you confer, support your writers by taking a look at how they are approximating the skills you have taught. When you think a child is ready to increase the sophistication with which she uses a skill, consult your skill ladder to choose what to teach next. This will help you move the child along successfully, instead of teaching ten steps ahead and losing the child in the process.

Work with your colleagues to add to these skill ladders:

Making Characters Talk

▶ Draw a speech bubble and fill in the words. This can show what someone is saying.

▶ Add the exact words that a person said in quotations. (e.g.: "My mom said, 'No way'.")

▶ Write exactly what a character said. After writing what the character said, write what the character did.

▶ Make characters talk back and forth.

Putting Spaces Between Words

▶ Say the sentence. Then say it again, and this time, draw a line for each word you plan to write. Now touch the lines you've drawn, and as you touch each one, name the word you'll write there. Then write a word on each line.

▶ Use a divider to remind you to leave space between words. The divider can be your finger. After writing a word, put your finger onto the page, and begin the next word after leaving a fingerful of space. (Some teachers go so far as to help children make spacers from craft sticks—children decorate their stick, call it Spaceman, and place it after each word to help make the spaces.)

▶ Listen to all the sounds in a word as you write it. When you hear no more sounds, leave a blank spot (a space) to show there are no more sounds.

Getting Words on the Page

▶ Label the main things in your picture.

▶ Label as much as you can in the picture.

▶ Label the picture being sure you hear all the sounds in each word. Reread your labels after you write them to make sure you put all the sounds you hear in a word onto the page.

▶ Write a sentence at the bottom of the page.

Using Learning Scaffolds

I recall a particularly memorable parent-teacher conference with the father of one of my first graders, Johanna. I was really impressed with the story he told me about teaching his six-year-old to ride a two-wheeler. After taking the training wheels off her bike, he slid onto the back of her banana seat and put her on the seat in front of him. "Ride, Johanna, and I'll do the balancing for you." Johanna was nervous, but she trusted her dad, so she didn't say anything. After a week of riding together, Johanna's dad felt she was ready for the next step. "Climb on by yourself, Johanna, and I'll help you balance by holding the back of the seat." Johanna was nervous, but she trusted her dad, so she didn't say anything. "OK, kiddo, I'm going to let go—just keep pedaling!" This time she couldn't stay quiet. "No, Dad, *don't*—I'll fall!" But Johanna's dad did not heed her cry—she was already riding all by herself!

Providing scaffolds allows children to learn any skill with varying levels of support. Johanna's dad gave her scaffolds each step of the way as she learned to ride her bike. By the time he let go of the scaffolds and, literally, the bike, Johanna was ready to ride on her own. Just like we can give children tips to help them work with a new skill, we can also provide different levels of support as children become increasingly independent. We scaffold children during writing workshop in three major ways. First, the structure of the minilesson itself is a layered scaffold. Next, the active engagement of a minilesson can provide different levels of support, depending on where children are in their skill acquisition. Finally, after the minilesson is over, we continue to teach through conferences and small groups, which give us the opportunity to coach our children into transferring strategies from practice to habit. These provide more individualized support for all of our learners.

The Structure of a Minilesson Scaffolds Learning

It is not an accident that minilessons proceed as they do. In fact, the structure of a minilesson starts with a very supportive connection to prior knowledge and prior teaching and gradually releases responsibility so that by the end of the lesson, children are ready to try the skill with independence. Let's examine each part of the minilesson briefly.

Connection

The connection starts our teaching in the most straightforward way. In the connection, we *tell* the learners what we will teach today. We lay the first layer of the minilesson scaffolding by naming the teaching point. In the model in Chapter 1, the teacher states her teaching point plainly: "Today, I want to teach you that we all can be like Desiree. When we, as writers, want to be sure that our readers learn all the things we teach in our pictures, we can add labels with arrows."

Teaching

In the teaching part of the lesson, the teacher models or explains the teaching point. Most often we do this by demonstrating the teaching point as we write a bit of text, but other times we do this by explaining or reenacting how another writer has used the teaching point. At this point in the minilesson, we *show* children how to do the strategy we are teaching. This is the heaviest of scaffolds, as the children do not try the strategy yet; instead, they watch and listen to learn. In our model, the teacher shows the children how she labels the picture with arrows. She thinks out loud and even pretends to get stuck so that some children will be working with her, even going one step ahead of her; as the teacher becomes unstuck, she demonstrates the skill children will try in a moment.

Active Engagement

In the active engagement, we peel away the supportive scaffolding to varying degrees (see the section that begins on page 29) and we give children a chance to *try* what we have taught. During the active engagement, children often support each other through partnership work, and the teacher mills around to provide additional support. The active engagement in the model minilesson is very supportive. The teacher starts by inviting children to try the teaching point as she repeats each of the steps: "Now it is your turn to try. Remember, look closely at the picture, find something we can teach people about Beatrice, and think about the label you would add with an arrow." One student shares and the teacher gives all children time to re-try the strategy after a second demonstration. She also has children talk to their partners to give each other added support.

Link

In the link we set up children to transfer the teaching point to their independent writing. We name the teaching point one last time and invite children to try it on their own as we send them off to write. In the model minilesson, the teacher reminds children one more time of the strategy they will try and puts that strategy in the context of their ongoing work, thus nudging them to try it independently: "So, writers, anytime you want to add more information to your pictures, you can add details like you have been doing *and* you can use labels with arrows to point out your details. Off you go!"

The minilesson is a very efficient scaffold. We make a connection, teach a skill and help children try it with support from the teacher and classmates, then send children off to work by themselves—all in ten minutes!

The Active Engagement Provides Extra Scaffolds

When we teach a new skill or strategy, sometimes we want to give our students a lot of support and sometimes we want them to try it with a little more independence. If children need more support because a strategy is new or particularly tricky, we tend to offer more scaffolds during the active engagement. In the model minilesson, the teacher adds scaffolds to the active engagement by using a supportive text. She has the whole class practice on a sample text—a mural that the class has created during science. Because this sample is familiar to the children, they don't have to take the time to get to know it. Also, because the children are all working on the same text, they can share ideas with each other about how to try the strategy. If the children were all trying the strategy on their own writing, they would not be able to draw support from each other as easily. Working with a partner in the active engagement also provides support.

Another way to add support to an active engagement is simply to have children try the strategy more than once. In the model minilesson, the teacher has the students think of one label, then she has a child come up and add it, then she asks the students to think *again* and come up with another label. She does this a number of times. Each time the children practice, they become more familiar with the strategy and more ready to use it independently.

Thinking Beyond the Model

In the active engagement, children try the teaching point or strategy. To do this they often need a text or idea from which to work. If you give them the text or idea, you are providing a little extra help. If you have them come up with the ideas on their own or work with their own writing, you are providing less support.

Here are a few ways to make an active engagement more supportive:

- Use the text of a published author children know well and have children notice how he used the strategy.

- Use a bit of your writing and have children try the strategy with it.

- Use a bit of student writing and have children try the strategy with it.

- Create a piece of shared writing that develops from one day to the next by having children try each new strategy on the same piece.

Another way to make an active engagement more supportive is to coach children as they try the strategy. With this method, the teacher gets the students started by talking them through the strategy, then letting them try it on their own. Take a look at the following example. Here the teacher is teaching the children that they can get an idea for writing by looking at the daily schedule that is posted in the meeting area:

"Writers, now it is your turn to try getting an idea for a story by looking at the daily schedule. Let's start at the beginning of the day! Take a look at the schedule. It starts with morning meeting. Close your eyes and think about our meeting this morning; do you have a story about something that happened during the meeting? Maybe you want to tell a story about how everyone came to the rug quickly and Tommy almost tripped trying to get to his rug spot. Or maybe you want to tell a story about figuring out who was absent with our sign-in chart. Give a thumbs-up if you have an idea." Some thumbs go up.

"Now take a look the next thing on our schedule, reading workshop. Do you have a story about taking out your book baggy? Maybe you will tell about a conversation you had with your partner. I know Alex and Ashley were laughing a whole lot at the book they were sharing—that could be a story. Turn to your partner. Tell any story that you have thought of so far." The children storytell.

Notice that the teacher doesn't just tell the children to try the strategy; she talks them through the thinking part. This is a form of coaching. She scaffolds the students as they get started and provides an overlay of running commentary that steers them to move progressively along through the strategy.

■   ■   ■   ■   ■

Teaching children what they are ready to learn may seem simple, but it requires a great deal of planning, watching, caring, and understanding on the part of a teacher. You must first determine what children are ready for, then you must find a simple way to teach something big, and finally you must provide scaffolds to assist your students as they take on this big work. The methods described here will help you to do all of these things, but don't forget all teaching must start by looking to learners.

CHAPTER THREE

Principle 2

Children Learn When They Are Engaged

If you can hold the attention of children,
you can educate them.

—MALCOLM GLADWELL

When you browse through a bookstore for a book, sometimes something special happens. You see the cover of a book and you are drawn to it. Then you read the title; it's catchy. Maybe you recognize the author's name and you are further intrigued. You flip the book over and read the back; it sounds good. You start to read the first chapter. The next thing you know, you are late to pick up your kids, to meet a friend, to an appointment. When a book engages you like this, you read it and then pass it on to a friend. Instant engagement is one of most important indicators of a book's success. If an author doesn't engage you, you won't stick with the book. Engagement is also one of the most important ingredients in making our teaching stick.

In the minilessons in *Units of Study for Primary Writing*, Lucy Calkins and her coauthors (2003) engage children in the work of writing. They hook children by telling them stories, by getting them to move their bodies as they learn, and by getting them to act and role-play. Let's explore these three kinds of engagement by looking at our model minilesson and then imagining more.

Telling Stories

Jody Smith used to teach kindergarten in New York City. Whenever I remember the scene in her classroom at the beginning of the day, I smile. Picture this: twenty-eight kindergartners putting away coats, taking books out of their backpacks, sharing stories about their walk to school, the room full of happy noise. Then something happens. "She's reading!" one child says, and every head in the room whips around to see that, indeed, Jody has taken her seat at the front of the meeting area and is slowly, intently reading aloud the title of a beloved picture book. By the time she has turned from the title page to the story's lead, the whole class is on the rug, riveted, listening.

We use stories to engage children time and again throughout the day in our classrooms. Stories are a powerful way to draw in anyone, especially children. Because stories hold people's attention, telling a story is a great way to engage students during a minilesson. This is why so many minilessons begin with a story. In *Units of Study for Primary Writing,* Lucy Calkins (2003) refers to the start of a minilesson as the connection, and it is hard to imagine a better way to connect with students than through sharing a story. Just as an author works hard to write a compelling lead for her novel, teachers work hard to plan a compelling connection at the start of a minilesson. And the stories we use need to not only grab children's attention but also set children up so they are ready to learn.

Using a Story as a Way to Make Students Famous

Teachers know that by spotlighting the work of one particular child, we can set out a pathway that other children can follow. Although children love to hear about famous authors who have done spectacular things, it is even more special for them to hear about a child whose work has taken the world by storm. Listening to what one child has done, students often think, "I could do that very same thing!" And if one child is famous now for his accomplishment, then other children realize they, too, can do noteworthy work. Stories that detail what a child did first, next, and next, and that chronicle not only the child's actions but also the questions the child asked herself and the decisions she made, can pave the way for others. When a student becomes famous for a particular strategy, lots of children want to do that smart work, to get a piece of the glory, and this makes the strategy stick.

In the model minilesson in Chapter 1, the teacher told a story about Jordan making a picture that carried lots of information, and that one picture led the rest of the students to find ways to make their pictures more informative. How proud

Jordan must have been that his work made such a difference! The teacher celebrated not only Jordan but also Desiree, whom the teacher described as a "smart cookie" because she invented the idea that writers sometimes use labels to highlight the informative parts of a picture. Imagine Desiree's shining face.

Imagine the small groups and the writing conferences you've led during recent writing workshops as a field of stories, waiting to be picked. Anytime a child has done something one way and then tried that action differently, achieving better results, you have a potential story. It could be that you prompted the child's improved efforts. That's okay—just delete your role when you recount what the writer did. Chronicle the progression as if first the child did something one way, then paused, looked back, questioned that work, imagined another possibility, and tried again, this time achieving better results.

There are other kinds of stories to collect, too. You can find lots of stories if you realize that anytime a child in your class runs ahead, trying something that you expected to teach soon, you can use that child's work in your minilesson. In the story you tell, again, downplay your role and give the child lots of credit. In our model minilesson, the teacher didn't say to the class, "I told Desiree to label her picture." That would have stolen the child's thunder and made the story less exciting. The good news is that this means you can sidle up to any child who could use a boost of self-confidence, teach and support that child so the child does some good work, and then chronicle the story of that child's work, making that child famous. This is good not only for that one child—it makes *all* children feel like they can succeed.

You can also make a child famous for her strong effort in the face of difficulty. To do this, look for children who are struggling. Confer to help children who are struggling to progress. The next day, tell the story of how these youngsters fixed their writing problems. Use this as a way to get your kids engaged with the hard work of getting themselves past the problem.

Here is a story I once used in a connection to a minilesson: "Nicolas had a hard time writing yesterday. He sat down at his table and tried to come up with an idea for writing, but he was stuck. He almost lined up for help from me, but then he said, 'Wait. I can help myself.' He remembered that he could look at the idea chart to help him come up with a story. Pretty soon, he was writing away. Isn't that incredible? Nicolas got past the problem himself! Today I want to teach you that when we are having a hard time in our writing, writers can use the charts in our room to get past the problem."

You can make children famous with stories from any part of the day. If a child does something noteworthy, stop the class for a moment to celebrate with the story of how the child did it. You can even make that child the class expert. Say, "From now on, let's all be like Nicolas and get ourselves unstuck by looking at our charts. And if you forget how to use charts, ask Nicolas, our chart expert."

Using an Intimate Small-Moment Story About the Class

Teaching will stick more when it feels personal, intimate even. Each of us can think of a time in our lives when a respected mentor looked us in the eye, making us feel seen, and then taught us in a way that felt personal. That sort of teaching lasts a lifetime. Minilessons are intended for the whole class, but when a minilesson really works, there is an aura of intimacy about it, almost as if the teacher has gathered children close to say, "Guys, I've been thinking about you all weekend. I have just one tip, one secret, I want to share with you." In a magical minilesson, the teaching doesn't seem as if it is for any ol' class; it feels custom fit to *this* class.

In order to create this feeling in your teaching, first you must tell stories well. To do this, do all the things you teach your children to do in their small-moment stories. You can use story language and tell the story step-by-step. You can draw out the important parts of the story, creating tension. Start with "One day our class was . . . ," or use phrases like "all of a sudden" and "just then." You can also use a storytelling voice to make this teaching even more compelling. Get quiet for a spooky part or loud for a sudden part. Use a few little details from the event to help children picture it. Use exact quotes. Tell how people felt. Make the stories a few notches better than what you expect your children will write. Your stories model great storytelling.

Sometimes you may tell the story of an "aha" moment when the whole class came to understand something, and other times you may tell the story of a time when the class felt confused. All of these stories draw children in and can set you up for compelling teaching.

Using Stories from Your Own Life

Using classroom stories is a great technique to try, but don't stop there. Just as children are drawn in by stories about themselves, they are also drawn in by stories about the people they know. My sisters, brother, and I *still* like hearing stories about my father as a kid! Your children will be excited to hear almost any story about you.

Think of a story that has relevance to your teaching point or to the strategy you want to impart and use your story to frame your lesson. For example, when I teach children that they can get an idea for writing from thinking about something funny that happens in their lives and telling the story of that funny moment, I illustrate this with a story from my own life. Recently, I told some kindergartners that their lives are full of stories. "Think about the tiny moments that make you laugh," I said, and then told them about a funny moment in my life. "Writers, I was walking down the street with my son. He was wearing his Spider-Man costume—he wants to wear that thing all the time, even though it isn't Halloween! As we were walking down the street, someone looked at him and said, 'Hey, Spidey!' Judah looked surprised and then started to laugh. We kept on walking and then *another* person looked at him and said, 'What's up, Spidey!?' Judah smiled again and started to skip. Then he looked up at me and said, 'Mom, am I really truly Spider-Man now?'"

See the chart on page 40 for some stories to watch for in your classroom and your life.

Using Gesture

Teachers do it all the time. We want to teach our children a song, and as we teach it our hands start to move. We sing,

Story	Teaching Potential
A child tries drawing something one way, then another, and another.	Use this story to illustrate the concept of revision.
A child makes a house of blocks—an art project—and it fails. The child rethinks, and returns to the work with a new plan.	Use this story to illustrate the idea that writers pull back to assess, make new plans, and then try again.
A child in your class explains something to a friend, perhaps showing the friend how to use a tool. The helper doesn't *do* the activity, but supports it.	Use the story to teach children that partners can actually show each other how to do stuff.

"Row, row, row your boat," and without even noticing that we are doing it, we tightly clasp our hands around an oar as we push it through the water. Then we sing, "Gently down the stream," and we start to make a wave with our arm. By the time we sing, "Merrily, merrily, merrily, merrily," our children are mimicking our huge smiles as we sway back and forth. "Life is but a dream," we end, and all the children follow as we place our hands together like a pillow and lay our heads on them as if to dream.

There is something about moving their bodies that helps children learn. When we add action or motion to our teaching, children often connect with it and learn more readily. In fact, psychology researchers at the University of Chicago have shown that often learners understand something through gesture or action before they can use language to express that understanding (Broaders, Wagner Cook, Mitchell, and Goldin-Meadow 2007). When children participate in making the gesture, they make a gross motor movement and this solidifies what they've been taught.

Using Gestures to Give Children Directions

Asking children to make a small gesture every once in a while keeps their minds and bodies on your teaching. These gestures help us measure whether students are actively engaged. In the teaching part of the model minilesson, when the teacher demonstrates and wants children to watch, she has them each put a finger to their eye to show that they will watch this part. Then the teacher asks the children to put a finger on their temple to help them think. In another part, she tells the children to put a thumb on their knee when they have an idea. These may seem like very small bits of teaching, but they help children stay on track throughout the lesson. In much the same way that the hand motions help children remember the words of a song, each of these gestures reminds children of their changing roles as the lesson proceeds.

Creating Gestures with Your Students

In many classrooms, children come up with these gestures themselves. You can think of the situations when gestures are needed and then ask your students to assign the movements. Letting children invent gestures gives them the added benefit of ownership. In one classroom, the children decided that if the direction was to listen, the speaker would tug on his ear, and if the direction was to watch, he would make goggles around his eyes. In another class, a student would show that she had an idea by flicking her hand open and closed to imitate a flashing lightbulb. As children imagine appropriate gestures, they often come to a better understanding of each direction.

Keeping children engaged is an all-day job for us. We don't use these gestures only during minilessons. We use them during read-aloud and math workshop and when we have community conversations. All day long, when we talk, we move, and that keeps us on track.

Using Gestures to Illustrate the Teaching Point

Gestures also help us make meaning. When you see someone slam her hands down on a table, you don't need to hear what she is saying to know that she is mad. In the same way,

Direction/Response	Possible Gesture
Think about …	Finger to temple
Watch as I …	Goggles around eyes
I agree.	Thumbs-up
I disagree.	Thumbs-down
Turn and talk.	Pull two hands inward toward your chest.
I have an idea.	Flicker one hand open and closed.
Write in the air.	Scribble a finger in the air as if to write.

using gestures to illustrate a teaching point helps children understand the teaching point while also giving them a way to recall it later. In the model minilesson, the students have gestures to go with the strategies they learn. The teacher teaches the children to tap their fingers on their thumb as they say, "Details, details, details." With this small action, she makes clear the idea that when you add details, you won't add just one, you'll add many. Sam invents the gesture of drawing arrows in the air with a finger to represent the idea that writers can add labels to their pictures. Letting kids come up with the gestures also adds an element of fun and ownership, both of which make children more likely to use the strategies we teach.

Using Gestures as Prompts

One of the fun things about gestures that accompany strategies is that they become nonverbal prompts. Once children know these gestures well, you can use them to coach children as they write. If a child is stuck trying to come up with something to try in her writing, a teacher or friend can simply mime the gesture that matches a strategy to try. Using these gestures as coaching tools is a great way to use a lighter touch when children are becoming increasingly proficient with a strategy. Gestures make for quick, easy, fun advice that tends to keep children working with greater independence.

See the gestures on page 44 that teachers and students have paired with strategies from *Units of Study for Primary Writing* (Calkins et al. 2003).

Strategy	Gesture
Storytell a story bit by bit.	Tell it across your fingers, touching each finger to accompany that part of the story.
Stretch out the sounds in a word to help you spell.	Pull two fists apart slowly, as if stretching an elastic between them.
Focus. Instead of writing about watermelon ideas, write about a tiny seed story.	Watermelon topics are hard to get one's arms around. Tiny seed stories can be held in a cupped hand.
Show, don't tell.	As you say "show," spread fingers wide beside the face; as you say "tell," tap your mouth.
Use a period to stop the reader.	Make a stop sign with your hand.
Zoom in on the important part.	Pantomime looking through a magnifying glass.

Having Students Act and Role-Play

My son *loves* to play pretend. One night, this was the scene at our dinner table: "Judah, please eat your fish, we want you to get big and strong." I tried not to sound like I was pleading. Judah did not respond.

"Judah!" I said, annoyed.

"I am not Judah, I am Sir Judah. I am a knight and I only talk to other knights!"

"Oh . . . well, then, *Sir* Judah, will you please eat your fish?" my husband replied.

"Are you a knight?" Judah looked at Rob suspiciously. I was tired, and I was glad to see that Rob had the energy to deal with this one.

"No, I am King Daddy, and I want to send you on a very important mission to slay the evil dragon."

Judah sat up in his chair, excited to suddenly have a play-mate. "Oh, King Daddy, I have my sword. What kind of dragon do I get to slay?" Judah held his hand out to show King Daddy his imaginary sword.

"I fear I cannot send a weak knight to slay this dragon. You must eat your fish before you go on this mission!"

Judah gobbled up his fish.

Little children love to pretend and act. When they are very young, they wear costumes long after Halloween is over. As they get a bit older, they turn school and store into make-believe play, pretending to do the jobs they see the adults around them doing. On the playground, they take on roles. "You be the troll and you try to grab me as I go over the bridge." All of these games are centered on young children's love of acting and drama. In fact, we know that children often learn and express understanding in their imaginative play first. Erik Erikson, one of the most important thinkers in the field of psychology, claims that "imaginative play is a precursor of conceptual thought—in which possibilities are explored upon the inner 'stage' of a child's imagination" (1993, 67).

We can draw on children's love of acting and pretending to help us teach. By having children play the parts of the characters in their writing, act out new words, or pretend to be the teacher in a partner conversation, we can tap into their wonderful imaginations and use those imaginations to help students write.

Children Can Play Roles in the Minilesson

"I'll be the teacher!" People who spend time with children hear this phrase all the time; it is a major part of imaginative play. It is also a great way to get children engaged. During the active engagement, we often ask children to take turns as they try out a strategy with a partner. In order to keep the listening child attentive, you can encourage him to "be the teacher." As one child tries the strategy, the other child can act as the teacher, coaching his partner. I do this all the time in classrooms, and children have a lot of fun with it. The fun keeps them engaged, and the engagement helps me teach the strategy at hand. In the following example, I am using the active engagement to teach children to stretch out the sounds of a word while spelling. I ask one partner to be the writer trying to spell a word and the other to act as the teacher, coaching the writer as she spells. The children are labeling a picture of the gym and begin by labeling the adult in the picture with the word *coach*. Listen in:

> "Let's try labeling the grown-up in the gym by writing the word *coach* over her head, OK? One partner will need to be the teacher and the other will be the writer. First the writer needs to say *coach* slowly and listen to the sounds you hear at the start of the word. Write those down, then reread with your finger to see how many more sounds you hear, and record. Do this now."
>
> "I'll be the teacher!" Gabby says immediately. "Now, Johnny, say *coach* really slow."

"Cccccoach." Johnny looks at Gabby and then says, "K!" and writes it on his whiteboard. "Coooooach." Johnny writes an *o* and looks at Gabby. He looks stuck.

"Umm . . ." Gabby looks around for what to do next. She sees another partnership and then says, "Reread with your finger!"

"Oh yeah!" Johnny puts his finger under his word. "K-O-chchchchchch." He writes "ch."

Soon I stop the children and ask them to switch roles and work on spelling the word *basketball.*

By having the children in each partnership take turns role-playing the part of the teacher, we engage both children. By the end of this active engagement, Gabby and Johnny have each tried the strategy once, and, when in the role of teacher, they reminded their partner of what he or she could do. What's more, they had fun.

This is a great method to try in any minilesson that has children proceeding through a few steps. While we try not to have too many strategies that have steps, sometimes the best strategies, like this one, do. In my lesson, Johnny says the word slowly, then writes the sound, then rereads, and adds missing sounds. Because Gabby coaches Johnny stays on point while trying the strategy. Role-playing the part of teacher magnifies the stickiness of the teaching.

In a minilesson, you can invite children to assume the role of either the teacher or the writer. There are more possible roles, too. Many of the lessons in *Units of Study for Primary Writing* (Calkins et al. 2003) have children playing different roles as a way to engage them. Take a look at these examples from the volume on nonfiction writing:

- In Session I, children pretend to be graduates parading in to "Pomp and Circumstance." This prepares the children to take on a whole new kind of writing.

- In Session III, Laurie has a child pretend to be her husband as she shows children that trying out the directions in a how-to piece can help you find the confusing parts.

- In Session VIII, Lucy plays the part of a musical conductor and asks the children to be the instruments, calling out their all-about topics when, she, the conductor points to them.

Children Can Use Acting as They Learn to Write

Acting is an especially powerful tool in the writing workshop because when a person writes a story, the writer dramatizes the story in his or her mind, then recreates it on the page, so a reader can do the same. If a child is going to write about an event, he or she can not only recall the event but can go a step further and role-play it.

This method is particularly helpful when children are in the planning or rehearsal stage of writing. We often teach children to first storytell their stories to a partner, making them as dramatic as possible. This helps them write with voice and dramatic tension.

Acting is especially useful for young children because they are still developing their vocabularies. Often children can express an idea more eloquently through actions. By encouraging children to act and then talk about their acting, we increase their ability to communicate successfully. After they have done some acting, children can talk with a partner about how to put their actions into words.

When children begin to write fiction or scripts, they can use acting as a way to figure out a story line with a partner. Children act out the situation they want to write about with a partner. In this transcript of part of a minilesson two children in a first-grade class demonstrate how they use acting to compose their story.

Joey and Tammy walk to the front of the meeting area and stand beside me. "OK, writers, Joey and Tammy are going to figure out how our story will go by acting it out." I turn to Joey and Tammy. "Movie stars, are you ready?"

"Yes!" they reply in unison.

"Tammy, you are in line for the bathroom and Joey comes and cuts in line—action!"

"Hey, you cut me! *No* fair!" Tammy yells.

"Yeah, but I really have to go to the bathroom *bad*!" replies Joey.

"Well, I have to go, too. You can't cut."

"No, you have to let me go."

"No way!"

Joey starts to snicker and then says, "I'll give you a doughnut if you let me cut!"

Tammy laughs and replies, "You got a deal!"

In this example, Tammy and Joey used acting as a way to plan the story line of their narrative. They had not discussed what they would say or do in this skit before they performed it, but the skit laid the groundwork for the story Tammy later published. Just as we teach children to *tell* a story in order to plan, we can also teach them that some writers *act* as a way to plan.

Children Can Use Acting to Improve Their Writing

A child who is writing a poem about a tree may pretend to be a tree swaying in the wind in order to generate words for her poem. Another child might pretend to be his mother caring for him after he falls and thus discover that she is not just "nice" but also "soft and cuddly," too.

There are a number of lessons in *Units of Study for Primary Writing* (Calkins et al. 2003) in which children are encouraged to act something out as part of the writing process. The lesson Showing, Not Telling from "The Craft of Revision" is one such lesson. In this minilesson, Lucy Calkins and Pat Bleichman teach a group of first graders that you can make your writing more engaging by *showing* how a character feels, rather than just *telling* the reader. The children practice by rewriting the sentence "I felt sad." First, Pat and Lucy ask the students to pretend to be sad. Then, they all look closely at how it looks to be sad and come up with words that describe that emotion. The end result? "I walked slowly along, my head down, my hands in my pockets, dragging my feet along the ground." Acting is a very effective way to get children to play with language.

In the Checking for Clarity lesson in "Nonfiction Writing," Lucy and Laurie Pessah teach children to use acting as a way to clarify their how-to writing. Here, they teach children that they can read their writing to a partner while that partner follows the instructions they have written. In Sam's directions for how to do a somersault, he writes, "First you put your head down and your legs up. Then turn over." As Laurie tries to do the actions, the children see immediately that the directions don't quite work; Laurie is sitting on her chair, as she takes in the directions she tucks her chin, sticks her legs up, and then protests that she'll hurt herself if she turns over. Sam realizes immediately that he's left out an important step: put your head on the floor! This lesson feels almost revolutionary to anyone who has asked children to reread their writing and make it clear. All too often, children just don't see what is confusing. But Lucy and Laurie show us that by having children act out (or, in this case, watch others act out) their writing, we can help them find the confusing parts. Writers can use drama to help with many revision minilessons:

- A reader can show he or she understands a story by acting out the content of a draft.

- Writers can act out their writing and notice instances when their actions aren't yet recorded. They can draw on their actions in order to add more.

- Writers can act out an important part of a story to help them add more, making the important part longer and more interesting.

- Writers can act to help them add talking to their writing.

■   ■   ■   ■   ■

My colleagues and I have tried all of the methods in this chapter to get children active with the strategies we teach, to ensure that children do not just leave our teaching in the meeting area, but that they apply it as they write. I invite you to take the examples and methods here and to expand on them. Think about new ways of using story and gesture and role-playing to get your children active. Then let your ideas spread!

CHAPTER FOUR

Principle 3

Children Benefit from Physical Representations *of Their Learning*

What it needed was a subtle but significant change
in presentation. The students needed to know
how to fit [it] into their lives.

—MALCOLM GLADWELL

When I began this book, I carried around a notebook to record my ideas. The notebook is filled with bits of writing I worked out on the subway, ideas for outlines, little anecdotes I wanted to include, but it mostly contains lists. There are lists of smart things I have seen teachers do in their classrooms; lists of difficulties I wanted the book to address; lists of quotes about stickiness and learning; and—the one I have perhaps referred to most—a list of writing advice that friends, family, and colleagues have given me. This list includes advice like Don't check your email when you write; Never go more than two days without working on the book, you'll lose your momentum; and Read books you want your book to sound like. I have a lot of writers in my life, so the list is quite long. I love this list. It helps me all the time. When I sit down to write, I read through the list; when I am stuck, I look to the list; when I feel good about the writing, I read through the list—in short, I read the list *a lot*.

When we teach, we give our students writing advice. We say, "Try this!" and hope that our children have understood our advice and will now try it out. We would love for them to have notebooks filled with lists of our advice, but we know that just wouldn't be possible for the little ones with whom we work; they don't yet have the reading, writing, and note-taking skills to create such a learning tool on their own.

However, there are ways of recording our teaching so that children can access and use it while they write, much the way I have used my list. Here, I refer to these records of our teaching as charts and signs. Vygotsky uses the word *sign* for any artifact we make in order to remember something. In order for these signs to work, they must exhibit certain qualities. We must study how to make not only enlarged charts that hang on our classroom walls but also smaller, hands-on signs like table tents, personal learning lines, and strategy rings.

Making Signs That Help Minilessons Stick

A few years ago I was driving my nephew from my sister's house to my father's house for a party. Mizel was about three at the time and was already quite the jabber mouth. As we drove, Mizel peered out the window and talked.

First, he told me about day care and how much he loved his friend Justin. But pretty soon he stopped talking about his friend and started telling me about how he could read.

"Really?" I said. "That's great! What do you like to read?"

"I read signs," he said proudly. "I can read lots of signs. Like that sign says 'A&P.'"

I looked up. "Hmm . . . maybe he is learning his letters," I thought to myself.

Next, Mizel pointed at a sign that read "East Hampton High School." "That sign says 'High School,' 'cause Mommy works there."

As we drove on, he pointed at signs everywhere. When we passed his friend's house, he pointed at a sign that said "The Smiths" and told me it read "Xander's House." When we went past the Getty station, he told me the sign said "The Cheap Gas." And, of course, when we got a little out of town, he pointed at the golden arches and proudly read, "McDonald's."

Small children pick up on pictorial and even written language cues early on. When a picture, sign, or logo is connected to something meaningful for a child, he reads it in much the same way that adults read words. We need to take advantage of this fact. When we make signs to remind children of our teaching, we need to be sure that our students will read them and use them. All too often this isn't the case, and the signs we make just become wallpaper. There are four elements that make a sign a useful reminder of our teaching: the sign should reference your teaching, be simple, include pictures, and include words.

Signs Can Act as Reference Materials

When we make an enlarged sign on chart paper during a minilesson, we are making an artifact of the teaching in that minilesson. We commonly call these enlarged signs *charts*. When we make these charts, we are highlighting in a clear and often bulleted way the most important parts of our teaching. We then hang these charts in the classroom for children to look at as they write. Charts are meant to remind students of what they have learned; to answer questions they have; to help them out when they are having difficulty. These charts act as the reference materials that children use when they need to recall a bit of our teaching, much the way I use my notebook full of writing advice.

Reference charts help students by categorizing strategies, so that children know when and why to use those strategies. In our model minilesson in Chapter 1, the teacher begins a chart that will help children add information to their pictures. The title of the chart, "Ways to Make Our Pictures Teach More," reminds children *when* to use these strategies (when you are working on a picture) and *why* to use these strategies (to make your picture teach more). Then each of the strategies is listed, so that students know *how* to fill their pictures with information. (See Figure 1.1 on page 13.)

Signs Can Remind Children of the Where and Why of a Strategy

In "Authors as Mentors," from *Units of Study for Primary Writing* (Calkins et al. 2003, 50), Lucy Calkins and Amanda Hartman make a chart in "Learning from Angela: Writing

Comeback Lines." This chart uses column titles to show children where and why to use a strategy.

Where?	What do you see?	Why is she doing this?	We call it ...	Other books?
Joshua's Night Whispers	3 dots, 3 times	Slow the reader down, something more is going to happen	Dot, Dot, Dot	*The Leaving Morning* *Our Stories*

Charts like these draw our children's attention because they outline the important work that children plan to do. This gives students a sense of excitement and pride about their abilities as writers. It also makes them feel *very* grown-up. But we don't make these charts just because they make children feel important. We make them so that children can access our teaching as they write. A quick glance at the chart, and children are reminded of the strategies we have taught and thus are more likely to apply those strategies in their writing. These charts also provide students with a map of what they can do as authors and for what purpose; they know when to use one strategy over another. This allows them to say, "Angela Johnson used dot, dot, dot to slow down her reader. I want to slow my reader down, too, so I'll try using dot, dot, dot."

Charts Should Be Simple

When you are driving and you see a billboard, you take information away from that billboard very quickly. If you didn't, your eyes would have to be off the road for too long and you

Unit	Session	Title of the Chart
Launching a Writing Workshop	Session II: Carrying on Independently	When I'm Done
Poetry: Powerful Thoughts in Tiny Packages	Session V: Ingredients for a Poem	Strategies Poets Use
The Craft of Revision	Session IV: Revising by Taking Away	Writers Revise
Writing for Readers: Teaching Skills and Strategies	Session II: Examining Readable and Unreadable Writing	Easy-to-Read Writing ...
Small Moments: Personal Narrative Writing	Session II: Discovering One Small Moment	Writing Small Moments
Nonfiction Writing: Procedures and Reports	Session IV: Incorporating Features of How-to Writing	How-to Helpers

might get into an accident. Often advertisers use the familiar slogans or graphics from television commercials to keep billboards simple and easy to read. We do the same in our minilesson charts: we use the key words and catchphrases that we elaborated upon in our minilessons.

The chart from our model lesson has very few words, but those words are sticky: "Details, Details, Details" and "Label with an arrow." These names that the children gave to their strategies make those strategies fun and easy to remember. The simplicity of repeating the same words from the lesson helps jar children's memory just as familiar logos on billboards remind us of television commercials.

Charts Should Have Pictures as Well as Words

As soon as *Units of Study for Primary Writing* (Calkins et al. 2003) was published, every classroom I visited displayed versions of the great charts that those books suggested. The charts I saw were informative and fun, and teachers and kids alike loved them. And then something happened. The smart teachers with whom my colleagues and I work just instinctively started putting pictures all over these charts. Some said they were doing it to make the charts more attractive and others said they were doing it to point out picture strategies as well as word strategies. Very quickly, we came to understand that charts are doubly effective when they contain pictures.

When was the last time you saw a billboard with just words? It doesn't happen very often. This is because a picture can often convey a great deal of information very simply. In our classrooms, pictures add an additional support for our learners. Because many of our charts have words that children in our class cannot read yet, the pictures increase students' ability to read and thus use the charts. Here are two little rules: If your students read mostly books that have pictures, then your charts should have pictures. And, if your children use pictures to help them write, then your charts need pictures, too!

Take a look at the chart created during the model minilesson (Figure 1.1 on page 13). Here, the teacher uses a picture that the children have drawn and simply circles the parts of the mural that illustrate the strategies that have been taught. This is a very effective way to show how a strategy has been applied, thus making it easy for children to *see* the strategy at work.

More Ways to Illustrate Charts

There are three major ways that we illustrate a chart. First, we sometimes draw a picture. Don't be embarrassed if your attempts are a bit primitive; often stick figures and line drawings make for the easiest-to-understand pictures, and since your children draw in a similar way, they will not mind. In the chart in Figure 4.1, Danielle Michaeli, a New York City kindergarten teacher, gives her students step-by-step help in composing a story. Pictures enhance the words, thus making her chart clear and easy to use.

Children can illustrate the charts, too. One of the most popular choice time centers in many classrooms is the "Illus-

FIG. 4.1 *Line drawings are an easy way to illustrate charts.*

trate Our Chart" center. In this center, children come up with ideas for a drawing that will illustrate the strategies listed on the chart. So, if the strategy is *Write what the character is thinking*, the children may draw a picture of a person with a thought bubble or a person with a finger touching her temple. Children love coming up with the ideas for these illustrations and then seeing their work featured on a classroom chart.

Second, we can take photographs. Photos are a great way to engage children because children love having their picture taken. I like to take photos during the active engagement part of the minilesson as children try a strategy. The teacher in our model minilesson could have done this instead of using the children's mural. When Daisean and Noya walked up to add their labels with arrows, the teacher could have snapped a picture of them doing it. Snapping a picture during the mini-lesson always makes children value what they are doing. Emile Rosales, a first-grade teacher in New York City, finds that her children look at the charts much more often when they see themselves and their friends pictured there (see Figure 4.2).

Finally, we often illustrate a strategy by pasting up a piece of writing that uses that strategy. We photocopy a page from a student's writing, or a mentor author's book, or some class writing. We often use a highlighter to show exactly which words illustrate the strategy. Take the chart that we looked at earlier from the "Authors as Mentors" volume (see page 57). Many teachers have taken to illustrating this chart with pho-tocopied pages from the mentor author's books. In the col-umn "What do you see?" next to the words "3 dots, 3 times," teachers add a photocopy of a page from the book with the

FIG. 4.2 *Emile Rosales, a first-grade teacher in New York City, uses photos on her teaching charts.*

ellipses highlighted in yellow. In our model minilesson, the teacher used the class text to illustrate her chart. She photo-copied the picture that the class had drawn and labeled and used circles and arrows to pop out each strategy. In the chart in Figure 4.3, Lori Talish and Neika Wise, first-grade teachers of an inclusion class, make use of this idea to remind children how both a published author and a classmate used one of their nonfiction writing strategies.

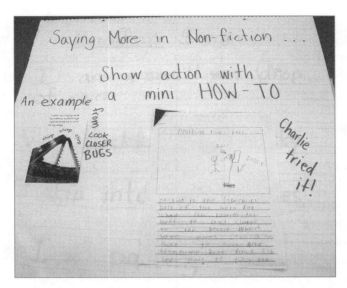

FIG. 4.3 *Lori Talish and Neika Wise illustrated a strategy with an example from a mentor and one from a child's work.*

Making Table Signs to Increase the Transfer of Learning

When I was a classroom teacher, the superintendent visited my classroom one day. She walked in and began to compliment me on the beautiful charts in my classroom. She knew I had been working hard to illustrate my charts. I was proud of my hard work and I loved being noticed for it. Then the superintendent walked over to one of my kindergartners and asked when she used one of the charts.

"Oh, I don't use that one. I have to make my eyes all small to see it, so I just use the charts that are near my table." Sierra smiled and puffed out her chest as she said this, proud to be able to talk to such an important adult. My heart sank. All my hard work and she wasn't using the chart anyway.

Even when charts contain all of the elements listed previously, they can turn into wallpaper. If a child looks up from her writing, needing to remember how to do that cool new strategy, and she has to squint her eyes to see the chart as Sierra did, the chart cannot do its job. We cannot allow large charts to be the only signs we use to remind children of our teaching. We have come up with two innovations to address this problem. First, we take the large charts that we hang around the room and shrink them down to tabletop and folder-size versions. Second, we make personalized signs that help individual students focus on the strategies they need most.

Make Small Versions of Big Charts

One way to make our charts more useful is to make them into smaller signs. If Sierra in my kindergarten class had a smaller version of the chart that the superintendent asked her about at her table or in her folder, chances are she would have used it.

Recently, I was working with a group of eleven teachers from across New York City. Our mission was to think about ways to make our classrooms run better. One day we started to talk about the issue of wanting to hang charts. Our challenge was that classrooms provided very few places where children could truly see them and use them without getting up. The next time we met, one of the teachers, Sara Ridge, was all smiles. As the meeting started, Sara opened her large teaching bag and pulled out what she called "table tents." Each was simply a file folder taped so that it stood up on the table. To these table tents she had pasted smaller versions of charts that had been up in her room. "I just reduced the pictures on the copy machine, and now the cluster of kids at each table has a chart right there with them!" We all oohed and aahed. Within minutes, we were running with the idea. We made more table tents, but this time we made them into flip charts using cardstock and library rings, so that any table tent could hold two or three charts and children could just flip to the chart they wanted (see Figure 4.4).

Over the course of the next few weeks, the idea spread throughout the schools. This was a little surprising because the idea was not *so* revolutionary. In Using Writing Tools: The Alphabet Chart, from "Launching the Writing Workshop" (Calkins et al. 2003), Leah Mermelstein and Lucy Calkins showed children how to use a folder-size alphabet chart to help them spell. But there was something about the innovation of the table tent that was fun, and useful, and sticky—everyone wanted to try it!

Edna Standerwick, a kindergarten teacher in Oyster Bay, New York, used table tents during her poetry unit. By putting poetry strategies within reach as her students composed their poems, she found that children tried many more strategies and used them over and over again. (See Figure 4.5.)

Many teachers have now decided that having one table tent for each subject makes sense. At the beginning of each

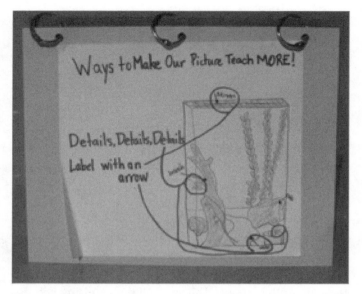

FIG. 4.4 *Here, the chart from our model minilesson has been turned into a table tent so that children can easily see and use it while they write.*

workshop—math, reading, writing—children take out the appropriate table tent and set it in the middle of the table. The large charts in these teachers' classrooms remain on the walls and are still used for whole-class teaching. Meanwhile, the students have easily accessible smaller versions they can refer to without interrupting their independent work to walk to the wall.

Here are a few tips for using and adapting table tents:

1. When there are too many charts on the wall, each chart can start to lose its value. Similarly, there can be too many

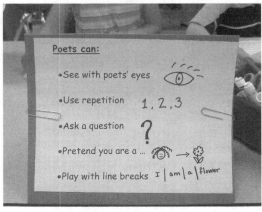

FIGS. 4.5a (top) and b (bottom) *In Ms. Standerwick's classroom, the charts start big on an easel for all to see during the lesson. But when the kindergartners return to their seats, table tents with the same information help them apply the strategies they have been taught.*

signs on a table tent. For any workshop, children should not be expected to refer to more than two or three signs.

2. Try to make the small versions of your charts look as much like the large ones as possible. Use the same wording, the same illustrations, and the same format. The more they look alike, the more they will support transfer of ideas from your minilesson to work time.

3. Retire signs with a celebration. During a share, you can announce that a sign or a chart is ready to retire. You might say to your kindergartners, "At the beginning of the year, I pointed to this sign every day in conferences with you. Let's read it together: 'We are *authors* because we write using: our names; pictures that tell a story; words.' Well, today I walked around the classroom, and I saw every one of you putting those three things in your writing without being reminded. Let's give ourselves a round of applause. Now we can take this chart down. Its work is done; it can retire!"

Make Signs to Differentiate for Individual Students

Those of us who teach writing in a workshop do so largely because of our commitment to differentiated responsive teaching. We teach a whole-group lesson for only ten minutes and then devote the bulk of our teaching time to the work we do with individuals and small groups. If we are going to make small versions of our signs, then why not make versions of these signs that make our teaching more

FIG. 4.6 *Johnny needed work on two strategies in particular, so his teacher made him a strategy ring to help him stay focused on the work he needed most.*

individualized? To this end, some teachers have decided to make personal learning lines or strategy rings for each child. This allows children to have an artifact that is as specific to them as a writing conference. So, Johnny has a strategy ring with "Label with an arrow" and "Stretch your words to hear more sounds" (see Figure 4.6), and Natalie has a strategy ring with "Use a known word to spell an unknown word" and "Add to your fact by saying why it is important." Thus each child has a reminder of the work on which he or she should be most focused. Kristen Larke, a first-grade teacher on Long Island, has even attached the strategy rings to her students' writing folders so they are easy to find and hard to lose (see Figure 4.7).

FIGS. 4.7a (top) and b (bottom) *A first grader refers to her strategy ring to help her write.*

This is a simple task. Start with library rings. Punch holes in index cards and attach them to the library rings. Pass these out to the children in your class. Have the children decorate and write their names on one index card. These index cards will soon fill their strategy rings. From here on, whenever you pull a small group or have a conference with a student, you can record the teaching point on one of that child's index cards. Perhaps you will even give the child a moment to illustrate the strategy, so that he or she can read the words and remember the work that those words signify. During writing workshop, this can be a tool that each child keeps next to him as he writes. As you confer, you may find that a student has mastered a particular strategy. This is cause for celebration! Compliment the student on his accomplishment and help him retire the strategy by taking it off the ring. In two classrooms on Long Island, Erin Huber and Coleen Brunken have made Accomplishment Bulletin Boards hold and celebrate all of the retired strategy ring cards (see Figure 4.8).

Some teachers use learning lines instead. A learning line is simply a list of strategies on a bookmark. Each time you want a child to focus on a certain strategy, you write it on the bookmark. Again, you may illustrate the strategies to make sure children can read them. Each time a child turns a strategy into habit, you can highlight that strategy. This allows you and the student to see which strategies she has mastered and which she is working on.

These signs make our teaching *super*sticky. When you sit down to confer with a child, you need only glance at the strategy ring or learning line to remember the repertoire of

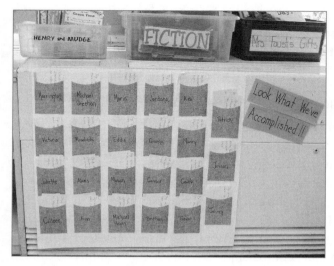

FIG. 4.8a *Colleen Brunken posts her students' retired strategies on Accomplishments Boards.*

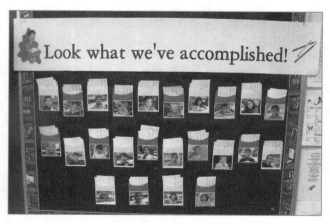

FIG. 4.8b *Erin Huber posts her students' retired strategies on Accomplishments Boards.*

strategies you helped her draw upon. A learning line might, for example say:

- ▶ Add a ground to your drawing and use it to show the story world
- ▶ Think, "What details matter to my story?" and add them to the drawing
- ▶ Show your changing feeling as the story unfolds in your facial expressions.

When a child says, "I don't know what to do!" you might make a flipping motion with your hands to prompt him to look through his strategy ring for ideas. Further, the child might open to one strategy card and reread each page of his writing, looking for a good place to try out the strategy. You can do the same with a learning line. All of these possibilities are simply ways to remind children of our teaching as they write, and thus help our teaching take hold.

■　　■　　■　　■　　■

Classroom signs help children turn our teaching into practice. When we make effective signs that refer to our teaching by using words *and* pictures, we help children apply the strategies we teach. We further support their learning by making big signs that we use as a group and then smaller versions of these signs to place on their tables. Finally, we can make personalized signs so children can focus their efforts on just a few strategies that we believe will serve them best. By physically putting our teaching in our children's hands, we are sure to make it stick.

CHAPTER FIVE

Principle 4

*Children Learn Through—and Love—*Repetition

To [children] repetition isn't boring, because each time
they watch something they are experiencing it in
a completely different way.

—MALCOLM GLADWELL

W hen I was on maternity leave with my first child,
Judah, my friend Wendy taught me to knit. As we
sat down to begin, I said, "What should I make, a
blanket or a scarf?" I thought I was being smart, starting by
knitting something rectangular so I wouldn't have to learn the
hard stuff yet.

"Neither," Wendy replied. "You are going to start by making a hat or booties. You need to make something that will go
quickly and then start another project right away."

"Why? Shouldn't I make something I want? Judah already has the hat and booties you made him, and those things are harder, aren't they?"

"Nope, both are easy to make, and if you finish one project and start another right away, you will learn to cast on (that's how you start) and cast off (that's how you finish). You have to start a project and finish it and then do another right away to learn casting. If you do a big project, you'll forget how to cast on and off by the time you start your next thing."

Wendy is a good friend and smart, too. This story shows how much she knows about teaching. If you learn to do something, but you don't do it over and over, chances are you will forget how to do it. We want our children to turn the strategies we teach into writing habits, but this won't happen if they try a strategy once and then never try it again. That is why repetition is so important to our teaching.

Using Repetition in the Minilesson

I love to drive when I know where I am going. On my way to my mom's house, I love to listen to the radio, especially National Public Radio. I get lost in the news and the stories about people and places all over the world. If I'm driving to the supermarket, I love to make quick phone calls to friends. When I drive to pick up my nephew at school, I love to play a great song and sing along, knowing no one can hear me. Driving to familiar places is great, because I can get there without even thinking about it, so I can use my brain to learn something, talk to someone, or sing along.

Conversely, I dread driving when I do *not* know where I am going. If I am driving to a new place, I turn my radio off; I turn my phone off; I turn my CD player off. I need every bit of my brain to navigate. I watch the road and road signs like a hawk. My eyes dart back and forth between my directions, a map, and the road. I am so fearful of getting lost that when I do arrive at my destination, I am usually weary from all the worrying.

The repetition of driving somewhere over and over again makes the drive so familiar that it becomes something we can do with great ease. Using repetitious structures and language in the classroom can do the same for our teaching.

Use Repetition with a Predictable Structure

Minilessons help teaching stick because they go the same way every time. The structure of a minilesson allows children to know and anticipate the rhythm of our teaching and to feel comfortable in its predictability. The structure of a minilesson becomes the road map, helping children anticipate how teaching and learning will go. Once the pattern is established, students approach a minilesson ready and eager to concentrate for ten minutes of focused learning.

Each minilesson has four parts: connection, teach, active engagement, and link. These four parts follow the same order every time and contain the same kind of teaching every time. When the structure of our teaching is predictable, children can focus on the *content* we are teaching instead of the *way* we are teaching that content. As in the model minilesson in Chapter 1, the students know what to expect and they also know what is expected of them. They can use all of their energy to learn the new content.

Use Repetition with the Teaching Point

One of the ways that the TCRWP has embraced the idea of repetition is that in our minilessons we generally repeat the teaching point approximately six times over the course of the lesson. This is something K–2 teachers at the TCRWP learned to do after studying the upper-elementary Units of Study books, bringing the more delineated structure of those minilessons into primary classrooms. Look at the model lesson again.

- The teacher clearly states the teaching point *once* at the end of the connection: "Today, I want to teach you that we all can be like Desiree. When writers want to be sure that our readers learn all the things we teach in our pictures, we can add labels with arrows."

- She says it at least twice in the teaching section of the minilesson. Before she does her demonstration, she states the teaching point again. She then closes her demonstration by stating the teaching point yet again.

- She says it *twice* in the active engagement. At the beginning, the teacher invites the students to try the teaching point, and then she congratulates the students on trying the teaching point—and states it one more time.

- Finally, the teacher closes the lesson by saying the teaching point *one last time*, reminding children to draw on this as the writers go off to write.

This repetition serves a number of purposes. First, it ensures that children know what we are trying to teach and gives them words to use when talking about that teaching. This is very important because when children agree upon a name for the strategy, this allows children to hold on to the text strategy more easily. Notice that the teacher used almost the same words each time she repeated the teaching point. Much like advertisers repeat slogans, teachers repeat teaching points over and over, therefore helping their teaching points stick with students.

The first time students hear the teaching point, they may not understand it, but when they hear the same words coupled with the demonstration, they gain a greater understanding. Then you repeat the words again and this time provide an opportunity for children to enact the words, and their understanding deepens. Finally, you can repeat the teaching point again, contextualizing it by reminding the children of times when they might try this work in their own writing. This layering increases the likelihood that the children will understand and therefore hold onto the strategy.

Repeat Familiar Transitional Phrases

Another way we use repetition in the minilesson is that each time we cite the teaching point, we use one of two or three phrases to set up the teaching point, cueing children into the fact that they need to listen carefully. The phrases that are used in the model minilesson are also threaded through a great many of the minilessons that my colleagues and I give to children:

- At the end of the *connection*, the teacher prefaces the teaching point with the phrase "Today, I want to teach you . . ."

- Before the demonstration in the teaching section, the teacher says: "Watch me as I . . ." At the end of the teach, she generally closes by saying, "Did you notice how I . . . ?"

- Before the children join in for the *active engagement*, she says, "Now it is your turn to try this."

- Finally, in the *link*, she says: "So, writers, anytime you want to . . ."

Each of these phrases is followed by the repetition of the teaching point. Of course, every teacher uses a slightly different phrase for each part. In *Units of Study for Primary Writing* (Calkins et al. 2003), Lucy Calkins often says, "Today and every day . . . ," instead of the phrase I use, "Anytime you are writing, you can . . ." The exact words are not important. What is important is that you try to use predictable phrases to cue your listeners. These familiar phrases will act like labels on a map, helping children navigate their way through your teaching.

Use Repetition in the Active Engagement

Over the years, my colleagues and I in the TCRWP have come to believe that when possible, it's ideal if the active engagement section of a minilesson can provide children with more than one oppertunity to try whatever we have taught. In the model minilesson, the teacher doesn't ask the children to try the strategy just once; she asks them to try it again and again. By the time the active engagement is ended, the children have thought of at least two or three labels for the picture. This gives students more supported practice with the strategy before they go off to try it on their own.

Using Repetition Throughout the Day

It happens all the time. You teach your children how to spell word endings like *ed* and *ing* in word study or in a phonics lesson, and then when they sit down to write, children don't use what you've just taught. You teach children how to use descriptive language during writing time and they do it beautifully, but when they are observing during science, their descriptions are not in the least descriptive. Children have a hard time transferring what we teach in one part of the day to other parts of the day. One solution to this problem is really quite simple: repeat yourself.

Children can turn new procedures into habits when they're reminded to do the new work over and over throughout the day. If we teach the same strategies and use the same language throughout the day, this can make our teaching stick.

Use the Same Strategy in Two Parts of the Day

You may have noticed that the teacher in our model minilesson uses a mural that the children made in science as the example in her minilesson. This is a subtle way to help children understand that what they do in one part of the day is connected to what they do in another part of the day. Clearly, if we want children to label their nonfiction pictures in writing, we want them to label their nonfiction drawings during science, too. In both places these labels will show what the child is learning, and in both places the labels will add to the overall quality of the work. So, when the teacher uses a science example in her minilesson, she is saying, "Do this during writing *and* during science!"

Use Repeated Strategies Throughout the Day

There are many times when our teaching will cross over from one part of the day to another. For example, if you are teaching your children about patterns in math, you might want to teach them about spelling patterns at the same time. If you are teaching children to write how-to books in writing, you might want them to also record the steps taken during a science experiment. Teaching the same concept or strategy in several parts of the day allows you to give children repeated practice.

Use the Same Language in Two Parts of the Day

We often use the same strategies in different parts of the day without noticing that we are doing so. And if we don't notice it, neither do our students. The best way to remedy this issue is to use the same language throughout the day. In the model minilesson, the teacher refers to children adding *details* as they observe and then draw the iguana's cage. By using the same language in both science and writing, the teaching is drawing students' attention to the fact that they are doing the same work in both content areas. By making this repetition obvious, the teacher helps the children realize that the experiences they have in writing can help them as they work in science and vice versa.

Here is a short list of skills and concepts that you can teach in multiple parts of the day and some language you can use to point out the repetition.

Skill or Concept	Parts of the Day
Add details.	*Writing*: Add details to make your writing come alive. *Science*: Add details as a way of observing with a scientific eye. *Reading*: Add details to your talk by giving evidence for an idea or theory.
Say the steps/story across your fingers to get ready to work.	*Writing*: Plan for your writing by telling the story across your fingers. *Science*: Say the steps to an experiment across your fingers to help you prepare to perform it. *Reading*: Retell the last chapter across your fingers to get yourself ready to read on.
Think about character feelings.	*Writing*: Add character feelings to your writing. *Reading*: Notice what your characters are feeling to help you think about why they do what they do. *Art*: Think about what your characters are feeling and draw their faces to match the feeling.

Using Repetition Within a Unit and from Unit to Unit

As I sat down in the teacher's chair, one of Lori and Neika's first graders, Calista, whispered to me, "What are you going to teach us today?" She wanted the inside scoop on the lesson I was about to teach to her class.

I bent down and whispered back, "I am going to teach you that you can use specific action words in your all-about books." A smile spread across Calista's face.

"Yesss!" she said with a happy hiss and did a little dance. "I was great at that in my how-to book. I bet I'll be great at in with all-about books, too!"

It is true, kids are not quite like adults when it comes to repetition. While adults often feel bored when they think they are hearing something *again*, most children are elated to learn something they already know. In writing workshop, one of the best ways we have for making teaching stick is to repeat the same strategies in different contexts. Some teachers worry when they find themselves re-teaching a concept. Think about how many times your youngsters have sung the same song, heard the same story—and don't worry about repetition!

Revisit a Familiar Strategy, This Time for a New Purpose

Many strategies can be used for different purposes. For example, sometimes we tell our children to reread their writing to make sure it makes sense; sometimes we teach them to reread to find misspelled words; sometimes we tell them to reread to find the most important part of their story. When we repeatedly teach one strategy, we can show children all of the many purposes for that strategy.

In the model minilesson, the teacher teaches her students to label. Labeling is not new for her students. In September, most of the children were not experienced enough writers to use sentences to tell their stories, so the teacher taught them to label their story pictures. Now the purpose for these labels is different. When the teacher repeats this strategy, she can be fairly certain that children will use it right away because they already have experience with it; the new teaching just gives them a new way to use an old technique.

Here are a few more strategies you can reuse for new purposes:

Strategy Used for One Purpose	And Another ...
You can make your characters talk to make your writing come alive.	You can make your characters talk as a way to start your story and draw in the reader.
You can act out your writing to help you figure out how your story will go.	You can act out your writing to help you find better words to say what you mean.
You can look at the word wall to help you spell the words we have learned.	You can use word wall words to help you spell new words.

Push Students to Use a Familiar Strategy in a More Sophisticated Way

When children learn a skill or strategy the first time, they often do it in the simplest way. If we teach *Say the word slowly and write down the sounds you hear* in the fall of kindergarten, chances are that the children will write only the first sounds for a while. A month or so later, the children begin to record the first and last sounds before moving on to recording all the consonants and finally adding some vowels sounds. All the while we are still teaching them that same strategy. This is because we teach children big skills. One of the important ideas behind this big-skill work is that children need to practice the same strategies over and over so that they can grow inside of a skill.

The teacher in our model minilesson is drawing on some big-skill work, too. The children in her class were taught only a week or two earlier that they could label the parts in a diagram. Even though the model minilesson teaches labels again, here the teacher is showing her children how they can use labels in *any* picture to point out important information, and thus she is expanding their use of the strategy. This kind of repetition gives children the opportunity to try a strategy in increasingly sophisticated ways, thus keeping the teaching fresh.

A Few More Words About Repetition

Before I end, let me offer a few more tips about using repetition:

▶ Just like doing smaller knitting projects helped me learn to knit by supporting my learning as I began a knitting project, did the project, and completed it, so, too, children need the opportunity to plan, undertake, and finish one writing project after another in rapid succession.

If you are going to repeat a strategy this month that you taught last month, pull out the old sign or chart. Make it clear to the kids that you are suggesting that they use the same strategy again, perhaps this time in a new way. Repeat pictures or symbols that you used on the old sign on new signs. This will help children use the knowledge that they have of the strategy from past experience and apply it in this new unit.

Periodically teach a repertoire minilesson in which you help writers draw from the entire repertoire of strategies, deciding which strategy to use. "Writers, I know lots of ways to add details. Watch as I read over my writing and think about which of these ways for adding details I'll use. . . ."

Use the same mentor texts over and over again. This allows children to feel really connected to one text and to see many different qualities of good writing working together in one text.

When you sit down to confer with a writer, repeat the teaching point that you worked on in the last conference and ask the child how her work with that teaching point is going. This holds the child accountable for repeatedly trying the strategies that you teach and prevents you from moving too quickly to new strategies.

Repeat the best compliments that you give to your students. Identify when a child is particularly good at something and then point out how that ability is useful in the child's writing every time you notice it. Repeat this compliment to the child, his caregivers, his classmates, and his other teachers. This helps the child build a positive writing identity and will thus cement strong writing habits and feelings.

In short, if it works in your classroom, do it again and again and again. Repeat the good stuff to your children; share it with your colleagues and with anyone who is ready to listen. The more we repeat our successes, the more successful we are.

■　■　■　■　■

Repetition is the final piece in the stickiness puzzle. It is just one piece—you will also want to teach what children are ready to learn, to keep them actively engaged, and to give them signs and charts to remind them of your teaching. By applying these strategies, you can make your teaching truly take hold. Real principles will help you teach in ways that make a difference. And what could matter more?

WORKS CITED

Broaders, Sara C., Susan Wagner Cook, Zachary Mitchell, and Susan Goldin-Meadow. 2007. "Making Children Gesture Brings Out Implicit Knowledge and Leads to Learning." *Journal of Experimental Psychology* 136(4): 539–50.

Bruner, Jerome. 1999. *The Process of Education*. Cambridge: Harvard University Press.

Calkins, Lucy, et al. 2003. *Units of Study for Primary Writing*. 7 vols. Portsmouth, NH: *first*hand, Heinemann.

Erikson, Erik. 1993. *Childhood and Society*. New York: W.W. Norton and Company.

Gladwell, Malcolm. 2002. *The Tipping Point*. New York: Little, Brown.

Jones, Susan. 1999. "Grow a Brain!" Retrieved June 1, 2008, www.susanjjones.com/movement.pdf.

Vygotsky, Lev. 1978. *Mind in Society: Development of Higher Psychological Processes*. 14th ed. Cambridge: Harvard University Press.

BOOKS RECOMMENDED
BY THIS AUTHOR

Here is a brief list of books about writing workshop that you might want to look at after reading this text:

Bomer, Katherine. 2005. *Writing a Life: Teaching Memoir to Sharpen Insight, Shape Meaning—and Triumph Over Tests.* Portsmouth, NH: Heinemann.

Calkins, Lucy. 1994. *The Art of Teaching Writing.* Portsmouth, NH: Heinemann.

Calkins, Lucy, Amanda Hartman, and Zoe Ryder White. 2005. *One to One: The Art of Conferring with Young Writers.* Portsmouth, NH: Heinemann.

Calkins, Lucy, et al. 2003. *Units of Study for Primary Writing.* 7 vols. Portsmouth, NH: *first*hand, Heinemann.

Graves, Donald. 1994. *A Fresh Look at Writing.* Portsmouth, NH: Heinemann.

Heard, Georgia. 2002. *The Revision Toolbox: Teaching Techniques That Work.* Portsmouth, NH: Heinemann.

Parsons, Stephanie. 2005. *First Grade Writers: Units of Study to Help Children Plan, Organize, and Structure Their Ideas.* Portsmouth, NH: Heinemann.

———. 2007. *Second Grade Writers: Units of Study to Help Children Focus on Audience and Purpose.* Portsmouth, NH: Heinemann.

Ray, Katie Wood. 1999. *Wondrous Words: Writers and Writing in the Elementary Classroom.* Urbana, IL: National Council of Teachers of English.